PSALM 23

(in other words)

Text and illustrations by

PENN KETCHUM

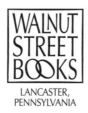

WALNUT STREET BOOKS

LANCASTER,
PENNSYLVANIA

walnutstreetbooks.com

Page design by Cliff Snyder
Cover design by Mike Bond and Cliff Snyder

Photo credits—Page 5— Mark Pontz; Page 7—Jason Hugg; page 44—Aimee Ketchum.

The text of Psalm 23 is inspired by the King James Version of the Bible.

Psalm 23 (in other words)
Copyright © 2019 by Penn Ketchum

Hardcover: 9781947597280
PDF: 9781947597297
EPUB: 9781947597303
Kindle: 9781947597310

Library of Congress Control Number: Data available.

Psalm 23 (in other words) is published by Walnut Street Books, Lancaster, Pennsylvania

info@walnutstreetbooks.com

About This Book

Psalm 23 is a beautiful prayer that
gives voice to our trust in God.
I wrote this book as a meditation on
the prayer, but using regular words
and phrases — the way we talk.

I also left space for **you** to write in your
own *"other words"* if you want to.

Running On Empty

The idea came to me as I was running south on Clay Road. My legs hurt, my feet hurt, I was hungry, and I had long ago emptied my water bottle. To calm my mind I was reciting songs in time with my footsteps. I repeated "Tangled Up in Blue" by Bob Dylan because it has a lot of verses. Completing it got me further down the road than a shorter lyric. I also recited prayers. I often did that—still do—to get me through some of the more challenging sections of a given run. It works.

Penn Ketchum

Finding New Words

I always thought, as I repeated some of those prayers, that they use strange words. Words I never used. I understood what they meant. I knew their literal meaning, but their strangeness blocked me from

> *"Whether you are an accomplished theologian, a devout churchgoer, or a lost sailor like me, I invite you to spend some time with Psalm 23."*

really connecting with the power of the prayer. I tried to see if I could recite the whole Lord's Prayer, for example, without using any of its original vocabulary.

I tried additional prayers to see what new meanings they might reveal to me. I began to have fresh insights into prayers that I had been saying without thinking since I was a boy.

These are powerful prayers to begin with. But I liked the insights that were coming to me with this additional practice. So I've put this book together for just that reason—to invite reflection on a prayer.

Your "Other Words"?

Whether you are an accomplished theologian, a devout churchgoer, or a lost sailor like me, I invite you to spend some time with Psalm 23. I offer here, with the deepest humility, some of my own thoughts on this prayer. Join me with your own reflections and see what comes.

> *"I offer this book as an invitation to look at this particular prayer differently. To look at it in other words. Doing this might shine a light on a whole new way of connecting to the prayer, or even to prayer in general."*

Why Psalm 23?

Many people, when reminded of Psalm 23's opening phrase, remark, "Oh, yeah, the funeral prayer, right?" Cracks me up. Yes, it's a passage often used at funerals. But that's a really wild and slightly misguided understatement. This is a prayer for the struggle, and as we know—what's more present than the *daily* struggle? We may often succeed, but for sure there is a *daily* fail. It can be a painful certain mistake. Or it can be as simple as not living up to being the person we hope to be.

Everyone's Dealing with Something

Sometimes our daily struggle is more serious—a fight with a loved one, a bad day at a job you hate, or whatever. I believe the old expression that everyone you meet is dealing with something. Something that's possibly painful. Even suffering.

Many people turn to their faith to help them find their daily strength or their balance. Prayer, for me, puts me in touch with my faith. Prayer sometimes helps me talk myself back into believing that it's gonna be okay. Prayer sometimes helps me get back to my faith when I'm drifting.

But I also know that many good, smart, wonderful people do not know faith. They do not enjoy the power of prayer. That's just how it is. Not good or bad or anything. Just how it played out for them. I offer this book as an invitation to look at this particular prayer differently. To look at it with *other words*. Doing that might shine a

> *"This is a prayer for the struggle, and as we know— what's more present than the daily struggle?"*

light on a whole new way of connecting to the prayer, or even to prayer in general.

And for the faithful, we fight on. We do our best, but it can be exhausting. As I've spent more time with this prayer, I've begun to see it as an outline of my faith, a comfort in the chaos.

Even When I'm Afraid

Don't get me wrong, I like when life gets weird, but I also get scared sometimes. When I feel that fear, I know to check my faith. And Psalm 23 is the perfect vehicle for doing that.

I hope you know peace. And if this book prompts some reflection and helps give voice to your trust in God, then great. And if it doesn't, that's okay too. Because like the Psalm says, ". . . Even though it can be tough. . . Never alone."

Penn getting ready for another Triathlon.

About the Illustrations

Both of my parents have always encouraged me to draw. My father is an artist and an obvious influence on my work. I've also been influenced by Don Martin of *Mad Magazine* fame, Picasso of course, Banksy, and all the unknown artists who tagged the New York City buildings and subways of my youth.

> *"Look for a few common themes in my drawings in this book—the Trinity, the infinity circle, the common struggle of humanity."*

Three Blocks, Three Circles . . .

Look for a few common themes in my drawings in this book—the Trinity, the infinity circle, the common struggle of humanity. The Trinity is sometimes front and center, and other times more of a background element. For me, the Trinity represents the goodness, the gifts of God. It is sometimes clear and obvious, like when we have calm, quiet minds. Other times the Trinity is all but lost among the

"You will see that many of my figures are disjointed or in some cases missing entire bodies. Just like us. We're a hot mess, and we struggle every day."

many other shapes and distractions that make up real life.

There are circles in our lives, and I see them in these pages. They are intended to reflect the infinity of God's love and, in some respect, the mystery of faith. Much like the Trinity, they are mixed in on many pages with the day-to-day stuff that consumes our attention every day.

But at the end of the day, we are each trying to pay bills, fix things that are broken, and reckon with our own earthly problems. Every day. That has to be part of the picture.

If you're gonna talk about lying down in green pastures beside still waters, you gotta own the fact that where we live is sometimes a long way away from still waters. We work toward those waters,

and with God we can take steps in that direction, but we are just humans.

This prayer is powerful because we are so flawed. Not because we are anywhere close to perfect, but because we desire to move that way. We seek peace.

Psalm 23 understands that. It validates the struggle.

Some Missing Parts

You will see that many of my figures are disjointed or in some cases missing entire bodies. Just like us. We are a hot mess, and we struggle every day. But we're out here doing our thing, and my people that I have brought to this book are in the same boat. Good people trying to get along with what they got. Carried forward, when they remember, by the Psalm 23 prayer.

Psalm 23

The Lord is my shepherd

I shall not want

He makes me lie down
in green pastures

He leads me beside still waters

He restores my soul

He leads me in paths of righteousness
for his name's sake

Yea, though I walk through
the valley of the shadow of death

I will fear no evil for you are with me

Your rod and staff—they comfort me

You prepare a table before me
in the presence of my enemies

You anoint my head with oil

My cup runs over

Surely, goodness and mercy will follow
me all the days of my life

And I will dwell in the house of the Lord
forever

Amen

PROTECTOR

MY GUIDE

The Lord is
my shepherd

OUR
FATHER

LEADER

GOD KNOWS
STUFF

(To Readers of all ages– Add your own "other words and phrases" to this page, if you like.)

I HAVE
WHAT I
NEED

WE GOOD

I shall
not want

NOT
MISSING
ANYTHING

I'LL BE
OKAY

(To Readers of all ages– You can write your own "other words" above, if you like.)

STOP HERE
FOR GOOD EATS

TO WHERE
I NEED
TO BE

He makes me lie down in
green pastures

GETS ME
WHAT I NEED

SO COMFY
RIGHT HERE

TO LISTEN

(Write in your own "other words" on this page, too. Or you can doodle something instead.)

WHERE I
CAN REST

QUIET AND
SAFE

He leads me beside
still waters

CALM
YOURSELF

TO REFLECT

TAKE A LOAD OFF

(I mean, you don't have to but, if you would like to, you can write on this page.)

ANOTHER
DAY

FED AND
RESTED

He restores
my soul

READY TO GO

GET
BACK
TO IT

HAPPY TO BE
MADE WHOLE

(Take a breath. Relax. It's okay if you don't wanna write anything.)

TRUST THE
PROCESS

He leads me in paths
of righteousness for
his name's sake

HE DOES
RIGHT
BY ME

IT'S NOT ALL
ABOUT ME

THE ULTIMATE
GPS

(To Readers of all ages – You get it, right? You can add your own "other words" above, too.)

IN THE
DARK

EVEN THOUGH
IT CAN BE TOUGH

Yea, though I walk
through the valley of
the shadow of death

HARD
TIMES

WHEN LIFE
THROWS
SHADE

FEELING
ALONE

OVERWHELMED

(This is a judgment-free zone. We don't even insist on proper spelling.)

YOU GOT
MY BACK

I will fear no evil for
you are with me

I AIN'T
SCARED!

NEVER
ALONE

(This is where you can write in your own expressions of faith!)

YOU KNOW
HOW

YOUR TOOLS
GOT ME LIKE

Your rod and staff—
they comfort me

KEEPS ME
SAFE, I
LIKE THAT

I FEEL BETTER
WHEN I LISTEN TO YOU

SAVED FROM
MYSELF

(To Readers of all ages– Add your own words—or anyone else's—to this page, if you like.)

LET'S
EAT!

A SAFE
PLACE IN A
CRAZY WORLD

You prepare a table
before me in the
presence of my enemies

STRENGTH
IN WEAKNESS

THE STRUGGLE
IS REAL

YOUR GIFTS IN
ALL THINGS

(To Readers of all ages – You are loved whether you write something here or not. Just saying...)

I'M
WITH YOU

You anoint my
head with oil

SOOTHE MY
WORRIED MIND

FIX ME UP

#BLESSED

(I dare you to write something honest here.)

THIS
DAY

YOU'VE
GIVEN ME
SO MUCH

My cup runs over

GOD IS
GOOD

I HAVE WAY
MORE THAN I
EVEN NEED

GRATEFUL

(Maybe you should wait until the second time around, and then write something.)

IT'S OKAY
GOD FORGIVES

GOD DON'T
GIVE UP

HOPE

Surely, goodness and
mercy will follow me
all the days of my life

IT'S PERFECT
EVEN IF I'M NOT

"AND DON'T CALL
ME SHIRLEY"

I WILL KNOW
PEACE

ON THE
DAILY

(To Readers of all ages– You are good enough just exactly as you are. For reals.)

WALK IN
LOVE

ALWAYS AND
FOREVER

And I will dwell in
the house of the Lord
forever

TRUST IN
THE GOOD

HE NEVER
GIVES UP

(To Readers of all ages – Write something. Reflect. Give thanks. Hug someone!)

RETWEET

NO
DOUBT

Amen

WE
BELIEVE

AGREED

Yup.

Personal Notes

About the Author of
Psalm 23 (in other words)

Penn Ketchum is usually known as the founder and namesake of Penn Cinema, an independent circuit of first-class, multiplex movie theaters in Pennsylvania and Delaware, including two IMAX theaters. It is true, he is a movie nerd and has a passion for his customers. Just watch him in the lobby talking with guests, or listen to his podcast. There's no denying it, he is the movie guy. But there's more to the story.

Penn was born and raised in Brooklyn, New York, where he attended Grace Church (usually under protest, to be frank). He went

Penn with his family (left to right):
Aimee, Kayla and Marley.

to high school in New England, traveled to Grateful Dead shows all over the place, drove as a courier for midwives in Kentucky, backpacked in Africa, led wilderness trips in the Rockies, and eventually found his way to college in Pennsylvania where he met Aimee on the first day of school. By and by they began dating and were married in 1996. They now live in Lancaster County, Pennsylvania, with their two wonderful daughters, Marley and Kayla.

Penn earned a Master's in Public Administration from Penn State University and earnestly climbed the ranks like any good aspiring administrator. He began as a case manager at the Lancaster County Prison and eventually became Executive Director of the County Mental Health/ Mental Retardation agency (as it was known back then). He served for a time as the Acting County Executive, the highest nonelected position in county government.

Recovery

Penn's faith stems from his early days at Grace Church, but his faith was most dramatically influenced by his involvement with the 12 Steps. In 1988 it became clear that he was powerless over alcohol. After some struggles, pain, and brushes with death, he began a journey towards sobriety in early 1989. To this day, his exposure as a young man to the wisdom that he found "in the rooms" shapes his daily approach to life.

Goodbye Office Job

Then a combination of boredom, disappointment, and a string of unanswered prayers motivated Penn to pursue that idea he had about building a movie theater and leaving the relative comfort and safety of a good job.

Penn had no real money and no practical experience. But he had a clear vision, strong faith, and a tolerance for risk.

He is widely known for his community involvement and business acumen. In 2018 he was named Small Business Person of the Year by the Lancaster County Chamber of Commerce.

Discovery While Exercising

A number of years ago, Penn realized that his busy lifestyle, while basically healthy, had nonetheless allowed him to become quite overweight. He woke up one day feeling old and very much out of shape. He began a journey that would lead him to endurance sports, including long-distance running, Ironman triathlons, and other endurance races. Penn lost over 75 pounds and has since completed many marathons and triathlons.

Completing such events requires many long training runs. Penn finds a quiet peace on these long runs, which he usually completes by himself, relaxing in the solitude. This is his favorite form of meditation. It was on such a run some years ago that he first had the idea to write a book like this. And now you are up to speed. That's your Author and how he got here.

Penn reflects on which new movies to play next at his multiplexes.

Suggestions for Using This Book with a Group of Adults, Young Adults, or Teens

1. Which of the phrases of Psalm 23 itself stood out most to you?

....

....

Can you explain why?

....

2. Can you list some of the high moments and the low moments of life captured in this psalm?

....

....

3. Name three of the author's alternative ("in other words") phrases that you liked.

....

....

....

Why do you think you liked them?

....

4. There is a lot of poetry and contrast in the images of this psalm. Name two images that especially caught your attention.

....

....

What do you find striking about them?

....

5. If you were previously acquainted with Psalm 23, what struck you most this time?

....

....

....

6. Why do you think this psalm has been so beloved through the centuries?

....

....

....

Suggested Group Exercises

1. Break into groups and discuss Question # 1.

(In each group, ask the person whose birthday is closest to today to facilitate and to make sure everyone gets a chance to talk.)

2. Now discuss Question # 2.

(Again, the Facilitator in each group should make sure that everyone gets an opportunity to talk.)

3. Now discuss Question # 3.

4. In your groups, ask each person to share a personal experience (if she or he is willing to do so) which reminds them of one of the portions of Psalm 23. Find a way for the group to affirm each person after she or he shares.

5. Try to give a name to the various characters in the illustrations throughout the book. Should it be a fun contest?

6. If there is time, choose to share your responses to Question # 4 —

Same for Question # 5 —

Same for Question # 6 —

7. When each group is finished, have each person shake hands with at least three others in their group, and say "I wish you well."